STUDENT

FATHOM BIBLE STUDIES

the birth of the church
ACTS 1-8

FATH●M

A DEEP DIVE INTO THE STORY OF GOD

FATHOM: THE BIRTH OF THE CHURCH
ACTS 1–8
STUDENT JOURNAL

Writer: Sara Galyon
Editor: Ben Howard
Designer: Keely Moore

Websites are constantly changing. Although the websites recommended in this resource were checked at the time this unit was developed, we recommend that you double-check all sites to verify that they are still live and that they are still suitable for students before doing the activity.

ISBN: 9781501839313

PACP10510518-01

17 18 19 20 21 22 23 24 25 26 — 10 9 8 7 6 5 4 3 2 1

MANUFACTURED IN THE UNITED STATES OF AMERICA

CONTENTS

About Fathom

Fathom.

It's such a big word. It feels endless and deep. It's the kind of word that feels like it should only be uttered by James Earl Jones with the bass turned all the way up.

Which means it's the perfect word to talk about a God who's infinite and awe-inspiring. It's also the perfect word for a book like the Bible that's filled with miracles and inspiration, but also wrestles with stories of violence and pain and loss.

The mission of *Fathom* is to dive deep into the story of God that we find in the Bible. You'll encounter Scriptures filled with inspiration and encouragement, and you'll also explore passages that are more complicated and challenging.

Each lesson will focus on one passage, but will also launch into the larger context of how God's story is being told through that passage. More importantly, each lesson will explore how God's story is intimately tied to our own stories, and how a God who is beyond our imagination can also be a God who loves us deeply and personally.

We invite you to wrestle with this and more as we dive deep into God's story.

Welcome

This book is yours. Or at least, it will be.

This book is designed to assist you as you explore, engage, and wrestle with everything that you'll experience over the next four weeks.

Each week during this study, this book will be filled with Scripture, activities, and questions to encourage and inspire you while you work your way through the Bible with your friends.

While we'll offer suggestions on how to use this journal, we want you to truly make it yours. Fill it with ideas and prayers. Take notes. Draw. Write poetry. Express yourself! Do whatever it is you need to do to help you remember what you've learned here.

Let this book be your canvas for creativity and self-expression. Let it be a place for honest questions and emotions that you may not feel comfortable expressing anywhere else, because at the end of this study, this book is yours.

You can use it to remember and reflect on what you learned, or you can use it to keep studying on your own, to keep questioning and exploring. We've included two sections at the end, "Takeaway" and "Explore More," to help you in that quest.

As you begin, we pray that you encounter the majesty and love of God through this study. We pray that you dive deep into the story of God and creation, and we pray that you find peace and hope in these lessons.

The Fathom 66

Bible Genre Guide

ENTER ZIP OR LOCATION `▢`

Stories ♡
★★★★★
Showtimes: Parts of Genesis, Joshua, Judges, Ruth, 1 Samuel, 2 Samuel, 1 Kings, 2 Kings, 1 Chronicles, 2 Chronicles, Ezra, Nehemiah, Esther, Matthew, Mark, Luke, John, Acts

`TICKETS`

The Law ♡
★★★★★
Showtimes: Parts of Genesis, Exodus, Leviticus, Numbers, Deuteronomy

`TICKETS`

Wisdom ♡
★★★★★
Showtimes: Job, Some Psalms, Proverbs, Ecclesiastes, Song of Solomon, Lamentations, James

`TICKETS`

Psalms ♡
★★★★★
Showtimes: Psalms

`TICKETS`

The Prophets ♡
★★★★★
Showtimes: Isaiah, Jeremiah, Ezekiel, Hosea, Joel, Amos, Obadiah, Jonah, Michah, Nahum, Habakkuk, Zephaniah, Haggai, Zechariah, Malachi

`TICKETS`

Letters ♡
★★★★★
Showtimes: Romans, 1 Corinthians, 2 Corinthians, Galatians, Ephesians, Philippians, Colossians, 1 Thessalonians, 2 Thessalonians, 1 Timothy, 2 Timothy, Titus, Philemon, Hebrews, James, 1 Peter, 2 Peter, 1 John, 2 John, 3 John, Jude

`TICKETS`

Apocalyptic Writings ♡
★★★★★
Showtimes: Daniel, Revelation

`TICKETS`

The Fathom Bible Storylines

Create   1

Invite   I

Act   A

Redeem   R

Experience   E

Hope   H

Introduction to The Birth of the Church

Background

Tackling the story of how the church began can be a daunting task. It can appear even more difficult when we consider that the earliest gatherings of Christ-followers as described in the first chapters of Acts would not be a "church" in the way we think of that word today. This study comes from the Acts of the Apostles, written by the same author as the Gospel of Luke. Both begin with an address to Theophilus, which means "friend of God" in Greek.

Traditionally, the church is said to begin on the Day of Pentecost, a Jewish festival when people would already be in Jerusalem as a community to celebrate. The coming of the Holy Spirit as described in Acts 2 marks the beginning of a new community made up of followers of Christ who will live together and have their lives forever changed.

As the early church continued to grow after Pentecost, the people had to decide how they would live together. The early chapters in Acts paint a rather idyllic picture of the community in which these early followers lived. Resources were shared, everyone was cared for, and people devoted themselves to learning, praying, and sharing meals together.

However, as any group grows in size, logistical problems are destined to follow. At this point, we begin to see the division of labor amongst the leaders of the church. There were those who preached and baptized, and those who distributed the funds of the church and cared for the widows and the poor.

The road to becoming the church we know today was not an easy one, and in fact it was quite dangerous. Persecution of the early church happened for a variety of reasons, but the central motivation was the threat that Christ-followers posed to the power held by the Jewish leadership. Early leaders of the church were imprisoned, beaten, and killed simply for doing what they knew to be right and preaching the gospel.

For the church to finally become the global communion that we know today, it had to expand beyond its Jewish roots. While Jesus was Jewish himself, he came to minister to those who were both inside and outside of that community, like the Samaritans and the Gentiles. Philip the evangelist continued that work by explaining the gospel to the Ethiopian eunuch, a Gentile who would never previously have been accepted into the Jewish community of believers.

Fathom Strategy for Reading and Understanding the Bible

"The Bible is written for us, but not to us."

This where we start on our quest. When we read the Bible, we have to constantly remember that the Bible is written for us, but not to us. Understanding the original context of the Bible helps us ask the right questions when interpreting Scripture.

For the first steps in our process, we need to understand how each passage we read functions in context and examine the historical background. When we read a passage, we should ask questions about the era, location, and culture of the original audience, as well as how a particular writing relates to the larger narrative of the Bible. This strategy not only helps us understand a passage's primary meaning, it also gives us guidance on how to translate that meaning into our specific circumstances today.

Happy Birthday, Church!

Summary

The church begins with a gathering of people defining what they believe and beginning to learn how to live together. You will explore how this initial gathering relates to how we gather as believers today.

Overview

- **Sync** with what it might have been like to be part of this early gathering through the concept of either fire or language.
- **Tour** the text of Acts 2:1-41 to figure out how early Christ-followers came to be a community.
- **Reveal** new insights into the text through the practice of lectio divina and journal about your sensory experience.
- **Build** understanding of how the Holy Spirit is working in the church and in your life through an activity that shows how the Spirit is represented in Scripture.
- **After** the lesson, explore different representations of the Holy Spirit throughout the week.

Anchor Point

- Acts 2:4—*They were all filled with the Holy Spirit and began to speak in other languages as the Spirit enabled them to speak.*

Holy Spirit Clothespin Tag

How to Play the Game

1) Those wearing a red bandanna are "Apostles."
2) Those wearing a blank bandanna are "Opposition."
3) Everyone else is a Christian in the early church.
4) Clothespins represent the Holy Spirit.
5) The Apostles will try to attach as many clothespins as possible to the members of the early church.
6) At the same time, the Opposition will try to remove those clothespins.
7) At the word, "Go," the Christians will try to team up with the Apostles, while avoiding the Opposition.
8) When the Opposition removes a clothespin from one of the Christians, they must return it to the original pile of clothespins. Only Apostles are allowed to pick up clothespins from the original pile.

How did it feel to be part of the early church?

How did it feel to be one of the Apostles?

How did it feel to be the Opposition?

Word Jumble

If you need help solving any of the word jumbles in this activity, the following verses (from the NRSV Bible) will provide you with a clue for each word.

1.   Name of the book about the early church

2.   Acts 2:2

3.   Acts 2:3-4

4.   Acts 2:3

5.   Acts 2:17

6.   Acts 2:1

7.   Acts 2:11

8.   Acts 2:7

9.   Acts 2:14

10.   Acts 2:42

As you read the following passage with your group, underline any parts that surprise you and circle any parts you have questions about.

Acts 2:1-42

When Pentecost Day arrived, they were all together in one place. Suddenly a sound from heaven like the howling of a fierce wind filled the entire house where they were sitting. They saw what seemed to be individual flames of fire alighting on each one of them. They were all filled with the Holy Spirit and began to speak in other languages as the Spirit enabled them to speak.

There were pious Jews from every nation under heaven living in Jerusalem. When they heard this sound, a crowd gathered. They were mystified because everyone heard them speaking in their native languages. They were surprised and amazed, saying, "Look, aren't all the people who are speaking Galileans, every one of them? How then can each of us hear them speaking in our native language? Parthians, Medes, and Elamites; as well as residents of Mesopotamia, Judea, and Cappadocia, Pontus and Asia, Phrygia and Pamphylia, Egypt and the regions of Libya bordering Cyrene; and visitors from Rome (both Jews and converts to Judaism), Cretans and Arabs—we hear them declaring the mighty works of God in our own languages!" They were all surprised and bewildered.

Acts 2:1-42 (continued)

Some asked each other, "What does this mean?" Others jeered at them, saying, "They're full of new wine!"

Peter stood with the other eleven apostles. He raised his voice and declared, "Judeans and everyone living in Jerusalem! Know this! Listen carefully to my words! These people aren't drunk, as you suspect; after all, it's only nine o'clock in the morning! Rather, this is what was spoken through the prophet Joel:

In the last days, God says,
I will pour out my Spirit on all people.
Your sons and daughters will prophesy.
Your young will see visions.
Your elders will dream dreams.
Even upon my servants, men and women,
I will pour out my Spirit in those days,
and they will prophesy.
I will cause wonders to occur in the heavens above
and signs on the earth below,
blood and fire and a cloud of smoke.
The sun will be changed into darkness,
and the moon will be changed into blood,
before the great and spectacular day of the Lord comes.
And everyone who calls on the name of the Lord will be saved.

Acts 2:1-42 (continued)

"Fellow Israelites, listen to these words! Jesus the Nazarene was a man whose credentials God proved to you through miracles, wonders, and signs, which God performed through him among you. You yourselves know this. In accordance with God's established plan and foreknowledge, he was betrayed. You, with the help of wicked men, had Jesus killed by nailing him to a cross. God raised him up! God freed him from death's dreadful grip, since it was impossible for death to hang on to him. David says about him,

I foresaw that the Lord was always with me;
because he is at my right hand I won't be shaken.
Therefore, my heart was glad
and my tongue rejoiced.
Moreover, my body will live in hope,
because you won't abandon me to the grave,
nor permit your holy one to experience decay.
You have shown me the paths of life;
your presence will fill me with happiness.

"Brothers and sisters, I can speak confidently about the patriarch David. He died and was buried, and his tomb is with us to this very day. Because he was a prophet, he knew that God promised him with a solemn pledge to seat one of his descendants on his throne. Having seen this beforehand, David spoke about the resurrection of Christ, that

Acts 2:1-42 (continued)

he wasn't abandoned to the grave, nor did his body experience decay. This Jesus, God raised up. We are all witnesses to that fact. He was exalted to God's right side and received from the Father the promised Holy Spirit. He poured out this Spirit, and you are seeing and hearing the results of his having done so. David didn't ascend into heaven. Yet he says,

The Lord said to my Lord, 'Sit at my right side,
until I make your enemies a footstool for your feet.'

"Therefore, let all Israel know beyond question that God has made this Jesus, whom you crucified, both Lord and Christ."

When the crowd heard this, they were deeply troubled. They said to Peter and the other apostles, "Brothers, what should we do?"

Peter replied, "Change your hearts and lives. Each of you must be baptized in the name of Jesus Christ for the forgiveness of your sins. Then you will receive the gift of the Holy Spirit. This promise is for you, your children, and for all who are far away—as many as the Lord our God invites." With many other words he testified to them and encouraged them, saying, "Be saved from this perverse generation." Those who accepted Peter's message were baptized. God brought about three thousand people into the community on that day.

Acts 2:1-42 (continued)

The believers devoted themselves to the apostles' teaching, to the community, to their shared meals, and to their prayers.

Questions

What surprised you about this story?

What do you think it would feel like to experience the Holy Spirit the way the people gathered on Pentecost did?

The disciples were already gathered together when the Holy Spirit came upon them. Why is it important for the Holy Spirit to work through community?

REVEAL

You are about to hear the Scripture again. After, you'll have a chance to respond about what you would have experienced had you been present at Pentecost. In the spaces below, respond to the Scripture using the following as prompts.

If I had been at Pentecost, I would have seen . . .

If I had been at Pentecost, I would have heard . . .

If I had been at Pentecost, I would have felt . . .

If I had been at Pentecost, I would have smelled . . .

If I had been at Pentecost, I would have tasted . . .

BUILD

The Holy Spirit Is Described As . . .

A Companion: "The Companion, the Holy Spirit, whom the Father will send in my name, will teach you everything and will remind you of everything I told you." —John 14:26

Fire: "They saw what seemed to be individual flames of fire alighting on each one of them. They were all filled with the Holy Spirit and began to speak in other languages as the Spirit enabled them to speak." —Acts 2:3-4

Wind: "When Pentecost Day arrived, they were all together in one place. Suddenly a sound from heaven like the howling of a fierce wind filled the entire house where they were sitting." —Acts 2:1-2

Water: "'All who believe in me should drink! As the scriptures said concerning me, *Rivers of living water will flow out from within him.*' Jesus said this concerning the Spirit. Those who believed in him would soon receive the Spirit, but they hadn't experienced the Spirit yet since Jesus hadn't yet been glorified." —John 7:38-39

Now it's time for you to come up with something creative to represent the Holy Spirit. Use the following page and whatever creative tools are available, and get creative!

BUILD

Need some suggestions?

- Build a sculpture.
- Draw a picture.
- Sketch a cartoon.
- Write lyrics for a song.
- Compose a poem.

Whatever it is, make sure it represents what the Holy Spirit is to you.

Holy Spirit Photo Challenge

The Holy Spirit is described in Scripture in many different ways. This week take pictures of what you think represents the Holy Spirit. Share these pictures on social media with *#HolySpiritSightings* so everyone can see what you come up with.

What are some images that represent the Holy Spirit to you?

Cut to the Core

This week talk to your parents about their core beliefs, and share your core beliefs with them. You might be surprised to find out what your parents really believe.

What are three of your core beliefs?

1) _____

2) _____

3) _____

PRAYER FATH●M

Together as a class, pray the following prayer.

LEADER: Awesome God, we thank you for the Day of Pentecost when you poured out your Spirit on those gathered together.

ALL: Pour out your Spirit on us, Lord.

LEADER: Open our eyes to see the places where your Spirit is represented in our world—in the wind, fire, water, and comfort we experience every day.

ALL: Pour out your Spirit on us, Lord.

LEADER: May we remember all that Jesus was, is, and will continue to be, both for those early Christians and for us today.

ALL: Pour out your Spirit on us, Lord.

LEADER: Give us a passion for our faith, like the passion of the disciples gathered for Pentecost.

ALL: Pour out your Spirit on us, Lord.

LEADER: We ask all of these things in your name. **Amen.**

A Little More . . .

Q: What exactly is Pentecost? Was it some sort of holiday?

A: By the time of Jesus, Pentecost was already an established tradition celebrated by the Jewish people every year. It was marked by a harvest festival that would be held fifty days after the beginning of Passover and would last for one week.

Pentecost was also known as the Festival of Weeks because fifty days is seven weeks and one day after Passover. It was one of the three pilgrimage festivals for the Jewish people, meaning they would travel from their homes to Jerusalem to celebrate at the temple.

This festival was originally intended to be a time of joy and a time to give thanks for the blessing of the harvest. However, by the time of the Pentecost celebration described in Acts 2, it had also become a time to celebrate the giving of the Mosaic law and the first covenant between God and the Israelites. It's interesting to note that the arrival of the Holy Spirit, which can be viewed as a new covenant with God, came at the same time the people were celebrating the original covenant.

Trouble in the Early Church

Summary

This week you will examine what it meant to be part of the early church, and how the growth of the church caused problems within that community.

Overview

- **Sync** with the tension between individual and communal living through an activity that illustrates the problems each can create.
- **Tour** through several Scripture readings that describe what the early church was like.
- **Reveal** the similarities and differences between the early church and our current community.
- **Build** an understanding of what it means to serve in community through the testimony of a guest speaker.
- **After** the lesson, choose an activity that helps you understand the breadth of community in your church.

Anchor Point

- Acts 2:46-47—*Every day, they met together in the temple and ate in their homes. They shared food with gladness and simplicity. They praised God and demonstrated God's goodness to everyone. The Lord added daily to the community those who were being saved.*

Rapid Rock, Paper, Scissors

In this game, you will choose a partner and play a quick round of "Rock, Paper, Scissors." The winner gets to take a candy of their choosing from the loser. When one round is over, quickly find a new partner to play, and the game continues. At the end of five minutes, time will be called, and the person with the most candies wins.

Did you find this activity frustrating? Why or why not?

Did you think the distribution of the candy was fair? Would you have distributed it another way?

What did this activity make you think about the way we treat people in our community?

Community Resources

Life situations, for reference:

1. My family has two adults with full-time jobs, with health benefits and no debt.
2. My family is behind on all of our bills and won't be able to pay rent this month.
3. My family owns a house in a gated community, as well as two vacation homes.
4. My family is on government assistance and, though we work, we can't pay our bills.
5. My family has two kids in college, and one parent just lost their job.
6. My family owns our house and both cars, but we live paycheck to paycheck.
7. My family is homeless.
8. I am sick and have no one to visit me.
9. I am a billionaire.
10. I am in prison.

What was difficult about this activity for your group?

What did this activity make you think about the way our larger community distributes resources?

Group 1: Acts 2:42-47

The believers devoted themselves to the apostles' teaching, to the community, to their shared meals, and to their prayers. A sense of awe came over everyone. God performed many wonders and signs through the apostles. All the believers were united and shared everything. They would sell pieces of property and possessions and distribute the proceeds to everyone who needed them. Every day, they met together in the temple and ate in their homes. They shared food with gladness and simplicity. They praised God and demonstrated God's goodness to everyone. The Lord added daily to the community those who were being saved.

Questions

What surprises you about the way the first Christians lived together?

_____

_____

_____

_____

_____

_____

How would you feel if you were asked to sell everything and give the money to the church, even if you knew the church would make sure you had enough to live on?

_____

_____

_____

_____

_____

_____

Group 2: Acts 4:32-37

The community of believers was one in heart and mind. None of them would say, "This is mine!" about any of their possessions, but held everything in common. The apostles continued to bear powerful witness to the resurrection of the Lord Jesus, and an abundance of grace was at work among them all. There were no needy persons among them. Those who owned properties or houses would sell them, bring the proceeds from the sales, and place them in the care and under the authority of the apostles. Then it was distributed to anyone who was in need.

Joseph, whom the apostles nicknamed Barnabas (that is, "one who encourages"), was a Levite from Cyprus. He owned a field, sold it, brought the money, and placed it in the care and under the authority of the apostles.

Questions

What stood out to you about this passage?

_____

_____

_____

_____

_____

_____

Are there things you are hesitant to give up for God, the way Barnabas gave up his field?

_____

_____

_____

_____

_____

_____

Group 3: Acts 6:1-7

About that time, while the number of disciples continued to increase, a complaint arose. Greek-speaking disciples accused the Aramaic-speaking disciples because their widows were being overlooked in the daily food service. The Twelve called a meeting of all the disciples and said, "It isn't right for us to set aside proclamation of God's word in order to serve tables. Brothers and sisters, carefully choose seven well-respected men from among you. They must be well-respected and endowed by the Spirit with exceptional wisdom. We will put them in charge of this concern. As for us, we will devote ourselves to prayer and the service of proclaiming the word." This proposal pleased the entire community. They selected Stephen, a man endowed by the Holy Spirit with exceptional faith, Philip, Prochorus, Nicanor, Timon, Parmenas, and Nicolaus from Antioch, a convert to Judaism. The community presented these seven to the apostles, who prayed and laid their hands on them. God's word continued to grow. The number of disciples in Jerusalem increased significantly. Even a large group of priests embraced the faith.

Questions

Why do you think certain widows were being neglected?

_____

_____

_____

_____

_____

_____

How do you feel about the disciples saying that preaching the word was more important than "waiting tables" (or serving the poor)?

_____

_____

_____

_____

_____

_____

Use the Venn diagram below to explore the similarities and differences between the early church and your own church.

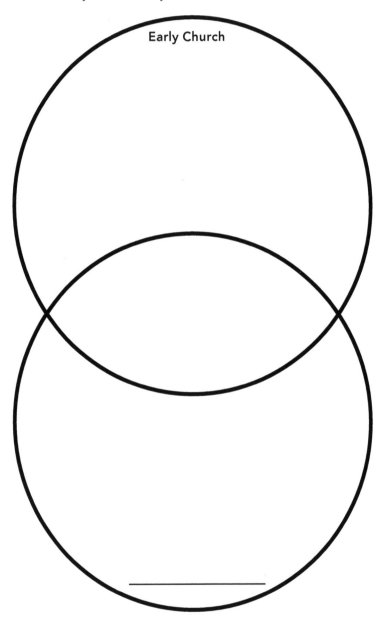

Early Church

BUILD

Use the space below to draw an outline of a person, and on that outline write or sketch different things a person called to serve God could do with their **brain, heart, hands, mouth, ears,** and **feet**.

#AllTheGifts

This week we learned about ways the early church lived together a long time ago. We still live together as a church today, and it takes a lot of people with a lot of different gifts to carry God's mission into the world. This week post a picture on social media every day that shows one of the people, places, or things that it takes for a church to do life together. Use #AllTheGifts.

What are three people, places, or things that it takes for a church to do life together?

1) _____

2) _____

3) _____

The Daily Community

Come and visit the church sometime this week so you can see all of the different people it takes for the church to operate. Record your observations to share with us next week, and take a selfie with some of the people you see working here this week.

Family Service

Talk to someone in your family and ask them how they serve the community. Ask them what they feel they are gifted at and where they would like to serve more. Share with them the gifts you think you have and what you might do with those gifts to serve God.

PRAYER

FATH●M

Read the following prayer together as a class.

God of all people, we thank you for those whose hearts are moved to serve others, and for those who share generously of all you have given them. Give us hearts for service and generosity, and help us to seek out those who are in need that we may do your work in our communities here and now, just like the early Christians did so long ago. Amen.

A Little More . . .

Then and Now

The early followers of Christ didn't worship in the same way we do today. We know that they met daily in the temple, which would have been in keeping with the Jewish custom of daily prayer, but they also would have gathered in homes for a time of rejoicing and to share a meal together. This was a big deal. In the first century, you only invited people to your house to eat if they could invite you in return. It would be like only going to the birthday parties of people who you knew you would invite to yours.

However, since the early church was holding all of their possessions in common, everyone—regardless of their social standing, class, or education—would have been invited to these fellowship meals. This challenged the way the culture around them worked.

When we offer an open table for Communion, we are allowing everyone to come and receive the grace and mercy that comes with Jesus' body and blood. We are daring to be as bold as those early believers. That's one way we've kept the traditions of the early church alive in our Christian practice today.

Power and Persecution

Summary

The early followers of Christ faced a number of problems, including persecution from different religious and political authorities. This week we'll learn about this persecution and explore issues of persecution around the world today and how we can support and pray for those who experience it.

Overview

- **Sync** with the theme of injustice by participating in an activity that illustrates how people can gain power over others.
- **Tour** through stories of persecution in Acts as you reenact the narratives of the early Christians and learn from each other.
- **Reveal** deeper reflections by reading articles about persecution today and journaling your thoughts.
- **Build** understanding of how to respond to persecution through a creative group activity.
- **After** the lesson, deepen your understanding of persecution with one of the activity options.

Anchor Point

- Acts 5:27-29—*The apostles were brought before the council where the high priest confronted them: "In no uncertain terms, we demanded that you not teach in this name. And look at you! You have filled Jerusalem with your teaching. And you are determined to hold us responsible for this man's death." Peter and the apostles replied, "We must obey God rather than humans!"*

Step Forward, Step Backward

Line up in a straight line in the middle of the room. You should be shoulder to shoulder with your classmates. Take a step forward or a step backward, depending on the following instructions.

Round One Instructions

1. Step forward if you have blue or green eyes; backward if you have brown eyes.
2. Step forward if your hair is short; backward if it is long.
3. Step forward if you have blond or red hair; backward if you have brown or black hair.
4. Step forward if you are over 5 foot 3 inches; backward if you are under 5 foot 3 inches.
5. Step forward if you are a good singer; backward if you hate to sing.
6. Step forward if you can play an instrument; backward if you cannot.
7. Step forward if you prefer math; backward if you prefer English.
8. Step forward if you prefer basketball; backward if you prefer football.

Round Two Instructions

1. If you have never disagreed with the government, step forward; if you have, step back.
2. If you have never argued with a teacher, step forward; if you have, step back.
3. If you feel free to choose your own church, step forward; if you don't, step back.
4. If you think the government supports your religious beliefs, step forward; if not, step back.
5. If you think your church is right about most things, step forward; if you disagree with the church a lot, step back.
6. If most of your friends believe what you believe, step forward; if not, step back.
7. If your parents belong to a different denomination than their parents, step forward; if not, step back.
8. If you feel relatively safe everywhere you go, step forward; if not, step back.

Did you think this game was fair? If you thought it was unfair, what do you think made it that way?

Today we're going to read about some of the power structures in the early church. Think about how what we learn about today connects with this activity.

Use the Scripture assigned to your small group to create your skit.

Acts 5:17-42

The high priest, together with his allies, the Sadducees, was overcome with jealousy. They seized the apostles and made a public show of putting them in prison. An angel from the Lord opened the prison doors during the night and led them out. The angel told them, "Go, take your place in the temple, and tell the people everything about this new life." Early in the morning, they went into the temple as they had been told and began to teach.

When the high priest and his colleagues gathered, they convened the Jerusalem Council, that is, the full assembly of Israel's elders. They sent word to the prison to have the apostles brought before them. However, the guards didn't find them in the prison. They returned and reported, "We found the prison locked and well-secured, with guards standing at the doors, but when we opened the doors we found no one inside!" When they received this news, the captain of the temple guard and the chief priests were baffled and wondered what might be happening. Just then, someone arrived and announced, "Look! The people you put in prison are standing in the temple and teaching the people!" Then the captain left with his guards and brought the apostles back. They didn't use force because they were afraid the people would stone them.

The apostles were brought before the council where the high priest confronted them: "In no uncertain terms, we demanded that you not teach in this name. And look at you! You have filled Jerusalem with your teaching. And you are determined to hold us responsible for this man's death."

Acts 5:17-42 (continued)

Peter and the apostles replied, "We must obey God rather than humans! The God of our ancestors raised Jesus from the dead—whom you killed by hanging him on a tree. God has exalted Jesus to his right side as leader and savior so that he could enable Israel to change its heart and life and to find forgiveness for sins. We are witnesses of such things, as is the Holy Spirit, whom God has given to those who obey him."

When the council members heard this, they became furious and wanted to kill the apostles. One council member, a Pharisee and teacher of the Law named Gamaliel, well-respected by all the people, stood up and ordered that the men be taken outside for a few moments. He said, "Fellow Israelites, consider carefully what you intend to do to these people. Some time ago, Theudas appeared, claiming to be somebody, and some four hundred men joined him. After he was killed, all of his followers scattered, and nothing came of that. Afterward, at the time of the census, Judas the Galilean appeared and got some people to follow him in a revolt. He was killed too, and all his followers scattered far and wide. Here's my recommendation in this case: Distance yourselves from these men. Let them go! If their plan or activity is of human origin, it will end in ruin. If it originates with God, you won't be able to stop them. Instead, you would actually find yourselves fighting God!" The council was convinced by his reasoning. After calling the apostles back, they had them beaten. They ordered them not to speak in the name of Jesus, then let them go. The apostles left the council rejoicing because they had been regarded as worthy to suffer disgrace for the sake of the name. Every day they continued to teach and proclaim the good news that Jesus is the Christ, both in the temple and in houses.

TOUR FATH●M

Use this page to make notes and plan your skit.

Acts 6:8-15

Stephen, who stood out among the believers for the way God's grace was at work in his life and for his exceptional endowment with divine power, was doing great wonders and signs among the people. Opposition arose from some who belonged to the so-called Synagogue of Former Slaves. Members from Cyrene, Alexandria, Cilicia, and Asia entered into debate with Stephen. However, they couldn't resist the wisdom the Spirit gave him as he spoke. Then they secretly enticed some people to claim, "We heard him insult Moses and God." They stirred up the people, the elders, and the legal experts. They caught Stephen, dragged him away, and brought him before the Jerusalem Council. Before the council, they presented false witnesses who testified, "This man never stops speaking against this holy place and the Law. In fact, we heard him say that this man Jesus of Nazareth will destroy this place and alter the customary practices Moses gave us." Everyone seated in the council stared at Stephen, and they saw that his face was radiant, just like an angel's.

Use this page to make notes and plan your skit.

Acts 7:54–8:3

Once the council members heard these words, they were enraged and began to grind their teeth at Stephen. But Stephen, enabled by the Holy Spirit, stared into heaven and saw God's majesty and Jesus standing at God's right side. He exclaimed, "Look! I can see heaven on display and the Human One standing at God's right side!" At this, they shrieked and covered their ears. Together, they charged at him, threw him out of the city, and began to stone him. The witnesses placed their coats in the care of a young man named Saul. As they battered him with stones, Stephen prayed, "Lord Jesus, accept my life!" Falling to his knees, he shouted, "Lord, don't hold this sin against them!" Then he died. Saul was in full agreement with Stephen's murder.

At that time, the church in Jerusalem began to be subjected to vicious harassment. Everyone except the apostles was scattered throughout the regions of Judea and Samaria. Some pious men buried Stephen and deeply grieved over him. Saul began to wreak havoc against the church. Entering one house after another, he would drag off both men and women and throw them into prison.

Use this page to make notes and plan your skit.

After reading the article assigned to you, consider the following questions.

What surprised you about your article?

_____

_____

_____

_____

How does your article make you feel about our connection to the early church?

_____

_____

_____

_____

Why is it important to discuss persecution when we don't really experience these same things here in the US?

_____

_____

_____

_____

In the United States, it can be difficult for us to understand a concept like persecution. However, around the world, there are very real cases of persecution happening every day.

Can you think of any incidents of persecution you've heard about recently in the news?

_____

_____

_____

Split into your skit groups again and use the space below to plan a skit that illustrates how you might respond to injustice and persecution in our society.

Everday Pray

This week pray for a specific person or group of people who are being persecuted. It could be from the article you read or it could be someone at your school who you think is treated poorly because of their faith, race, or some other reason. Write it down and pray for them every day. If it helps, consider writing your prayer out every day in a prayer journal.

Who are one or two people or groups you could pray for this week?

_____

_____

Worship Scavenger Hunt

Over the course of this week, take photos of all the different places of worship you can find near where you live and post them on social media. This will help you illustrate how free we are to worship in the United States since our churches don't have to be hidden from anyone. See how many different religions or denominations you can find.

Over the Generations

Ask your parents about what they think about issues of oppression and persecution. If you have grandparents or other family members, ask them about stories they may remember from the news when they were growing up.

PRAYER FATH●M

Wondrous God, we know you ache for those throughout the ages who have suffered for your name. We pray the comfort that only you can provide be upon those in our own time who are suffering at the hands of people who don't know you. Help those in power to show mercy to the faithful and turn their hearts to your love and justice. Move our hearts where you would have them go to show mercy and compassion to those in our own community who suffer because of their race, faith, or beliefs, and embolden us to stand with those who are struggling. Amen.

New Ears to Hear the Good News

Summary

The early church couldn't grow without apostles sharing the good news about Jesus wherever they were called. This week you will look at the story of Philip and the Ethiopian eunuch, which is a great example of going where God calls and sharing the good news of Jesus.

Overview

- **Sync** with the idea of a connected and expanding community through one of the activity options.
- **Tour** the story of Philip and the Ethiopian eunuch while discussing some of the important themes of this passage.
- **Reveal** your anxieties about sharing the gospel through an activity using journaling and prayer.
- **Build** on the theme of mission work by learning about missionaries from history and creating a talk show to interview them about their lives.
- **After** the lesson, participate in one of the activities this week to reinforce how God is calling you to share and serve.

Anchor Point

- Acts 8:36-38—*As they went down the road, they came to some water. The eunuch said, "Look! Water! What would keep me from being baptized?" He ordered that the carriage halt. Both Philip and the eunuch went down to the water, where Philip baptized him.*

Squiggle Line Tag

How to Play

1) When the game starts, you'll play like regular tag.
2) However, when the first person is tagged, they will link arms with the person who tagged them and they will work as a team.
3) From this point on, whenever someone is tagged, they will join arms with the person who tagged them.
4) Only people on the ends can tag others.
5) The game ends when everyone is part of the line.

For those of you who were "IT" first, how did it feel knowing you would eventually have to work to catch everyone?

When you were on an end, how hard was it to tag people and still remain part of the group?

When you were in the middle of the line, did it ever feel like you didn't really have to do anything but go with the flow of the rest of the line?

Domino Challenge

Your group will be given about one hundred dominoes. As a group, make the coolest domino course you can imagine. You can use other props to aid your course, but all the dominoes need to fall in sequence once the first domino is tipped over. You can't aid the course in any way.

What did you find challenging about this activity?

What frustrated you about this activity?

What would you do differently if you had to do this activity again?

Acts 8:26-40

26 An angel from the Lord spoke to Philip, "At noon, take the road that leads from Jerusalem to Gaza." (This is a desert road.) So he did. Meanwhile, an Ethiopian man was on his way home from Jerusalem, where he had come to worship. He was a eunuch and an official responsible for the entire treasury of Candace. (Candace is the title given to the Ethiopian queen.) He was reading the prophet Isaiah while sitting in his carriage. **29** The Spirit told Philip, "Approach this carriage and stay with it."

30 Running up to the carriage, Philip heard the man reading the prophet Isaiah. He asked, "Do you really understand what you are reading?"

The man replied, "Without someone to guide me, how could I?" Then he invited Philip to climb up and sit with him. This was the passage of scripture he was reading:

Like a sheep he was led to the slaughter
and like a lamb before its shearer is silent
so he didn't open his mouth.
In his humiliation justice was taken away from him.
Who can tell the story of his descendants
because his life was taken from the earth?

The eunuch asked Philip, "Tell me, about whom does the prophet say this? Is he talking about himself or someone else?" Starting with that passage, Philip proclaimed the good news about Jesus to him. As they went down the road, they came to some water.

Acts 8:26-40 (continued)

The eunuch said, "Look! Water! What would keep me from being baptized?" He ordered that the carriage halt. Both Philip and the eunuch went down to the water, where Philip baptized him. When they came up out of the water, the Lord's Spirit suddenly took Philip away. The eunuch never saw him again but went on his way rejoicing. Philip found himself in Azotus. He traveled through that area, preaching the good news in all the cities until he reached Caesarea.

Use the area below to take notes about parts of the class conversation that you find interesting.

REVEAL FATH●M

Use these questions to help you craft your prayer about sharing the gospel with others.

1. What scares you about sharing the gospel?

2. What excites you about the good news of Jesus?

3. Who are you worried about sharing the gospel with?

4. What do you feel like you need more of in order to be bold in sharing Jesus with others?

Write a prayer about ways you could share the gospel.

Samuel Zwemer

As an infant, Samuel Zwemer's mother prayed that he would become a missionary. During his senior year in college, Samuel dedicated himself to the foreign missionary service. Along with his missionary partner, James Cantine, Zwemer selected Arabia, the homeland of Islam, as his mission field because it was the most difficult place he could find. When no missionary society would support them in this difficult endeavor, Zwemer and Cantine raised the money on their own.

Trial and hardship were constant companions of Zwemer in the mission field. He lost several partners to illness and death, and two of his young daughters died of dysentery. Yet Zwemer was not deterred.

While some missionaries are remembered for the churches they founded and their many converts, Zwemer is not known for these things. After 38 years of mission work throughout Arabia, the Persian Gulf, Egypt, and Asia Minor, Zwemer produced merely twelve converts to Christianity. Yet conversion was not the ultimate goal for Zwemer. The man who would become known as *The Apostle to Islam* once wrote, "The chief end of missions is not the salvation of men, but the glory of God."

Zwemer passed away in New York in 1952 while recovering from a heart attack. Until his death, Zwemer remained a vocal advocate for mission work in Arabia and the Persian Gulf.

BUILD

Use this page to help outline your interview skit.

Where are you from?

_____

How did you get started as a missionary?

_____

_____

_____

_____

_____

Where did your work take you?

_____

_____

_____

Use the rest of the space to plan additional questions.

Amy Wilson Carmichael

Amy Wilson Carmichael was born in the small village of Millisle, Ireland, in December 1867. Her parents were devout Presbyterians, and her father was the founder of the Welcome Evangelical Church in Belfast. Despite this, Carmichael was an unlikely candidate for missionary work. She suffered from neuralgia, a disease of the nerves that made her whole body weak and achy, and often forced her to bed for weeks on end. Nevertheless, she was convinced to pursue mission work after hearing a speech about missionary life in 1887 from Hudson Taylor, the founder of China Inland Mission.

Carmichael initially began her work in Japan for fifteen months before moving on to a short stint in Ceylon (modern-day Sri Lanka), but she found her lifelong vocation in India. Much of her work involved young girls, some of whom had been forced into prostitution. When the girls were asked what drew them to Carmichael, they often replied that it was her love. The organization she founded would eventually become the sanctuary for over one thousand children. Carmichael herself often traveled long distances on India's hot, dusty roads to save just one child from suffering.

While serving in India, Carmichael received a letter from a young lady considering life as a missionary. She asked Carmichael, "What is missionary life like?" Carmichael responded simply, "Missionary life is simply a chance to die."

Carmichael died in India in 1951 at the age of 83. She served there for 55 years without so much as a furlough. Her biography quotes her as saying, "One can give without loving, but one cannot love without giving."

BUILD  FATH●M

Use this page to help outline your interview skit.

Where are you from?

_____

How did you get started as a missionary?

_____

_____

_____

_____

_____

Where did your work take you?

_____

_____

_____

Use the rest of the space to plan additional questions.

E. Stanley Jones

Eli Stanley Jones was born in Baltimore on January 3, 1884. After an early venture into law, Jones moved to Wilmore, Kentucky, to study at Asbury College. It was there, in February of 1905, that Jones and three other men were having a private prayer meeting around 10 p.m., when the Holy Spirit seemed to enter the room. As other students joined them, the revival spread across the campus and eventually the town of Wilmore. In his autobiography, Jones said that this revival prepared him for future work as a missionary and opened his ears to the Holy Spirit.

Jones graduated in 1907 and became a missionary to India. Jones began his mission work among the lowest class of people. He did not attack the dominant religions of the area, but tried to present the gospel without the attachments of Western culture. He also presided over "roundtable conferences," where people of all faiths could sit down as equals and share their testimonies about how religious experiences had improved their lives.

His reputation as a reconciler led him to become involved in many political negotiations in India, Africa, and Asia. He was a close confidant of President Franklin D. Roosevelt in the run up to World War II, and after the war, he visited Japan where he was greeted as the *Apostle of Peace*. He played an important role in establishing religious freedom in the post-colonial Indian government and became a close friend of Mahatma Gandhi.

Jones died in India on January 25, 1973. Upon his death, a prominent Methodist bishop called E. Stanley Jones, "the greatest Christian missionary since St. Paul."

BUILD

Use this page to help outline your interview skit.

Where are you from?

_____

How did you get started as a missionary?

_____

_____

_____

_____

Where did your work take you?

_____

_____

_____

Use the rest of the space to plan additional questions.

The Good News of Dominoes

The good news of Jesus is a lot like a domino course. When someone shares the good news, it can get shared over and over again, down the line. This week take one of the dominoes we used earlier and write on the back the name of someone who needs to hear the good news of Jesus this week. Over the course of this week, pray for this person and try to find time to share the good news with them.

Who will you pray for this week?

Called to Serve

This week share photos of places in your neighborhood or even around the world where you feel called by God to serve. Pray for each of these areas and, if you find an opportunity in your neighborhood, consider volunteering there.

What are a few examples of areas where you feel called by God to serve?

1) _____

2) _____

3) _____

The Family That Shares

Talk to your family about how they think we should share the gospel with others—how they share the good news with their friends; with extended family; with neighbors. What could you do as a family to share the good news of Jesus?

PRAYER FATH●M

Say the following prayer together.

God of all nations, we pray that you can relieve our insecurities and make us bold to share the good news of Jesus. We pray for all of the missionaries who are following your call in their lives and ask for your guidance in following your will in our own. Amen.

Takeaway

History is a funny thing. We often think of it as a list of dates and names that have nothing to do with us in the present, but by exploring it we can come to understand a lot about our current lives. Such is the story of the early church.

There are always powerful groups who will be threatened by new ideas or new ways of doing things. Through this study, you have learned how the religious powers in Jesus' time were challenged by the early church and the work of the Holy Spirit. Many of their boundaries were overturned in order for the gospel to spread and for new people to join the community that would become the church.

In the first lesson, you saw how the Holy Spirit moved through the community on the Day of Pentecost. It's so encouraging to know that the Holy Spirit is still moving through our communities of faith today! The Holy Spirit isn't just something we read about in Scripture; it breathes life into us and those around us every day. It continually shapes churches and forms us into a people who will do the work of the Spirit in the world.

We also know from reading these stories in the Book of Acts that when a new community forms, it doesn't take long before problems start to surface. Even within the Jewish community, there were Hebrew-speaking Jews and Greek-speakers. Sadly, the Greek-speaking widows were being left out of the distribution of goods. This led the group to appoint deacons who were called to serve others in the name of God and, by doing so, to show others the gospel. In the same way, today we form new programs and ministries to respond to the needs of others, but also to serve others while sharing the gospel.

In another lesson, you learned about the persecution of the early church. It was a dangerous time to be a part of this new community, and while we live in a safe place to worship as we please, that has not always been true for the church. Even today there are Christians being persecuted around the world, and we need to remember them in our prayers.

Finally, in the story about Philip the evangelist and the Ethiopian eunuch, you saw the need to continue to share the gospel with those on the outskirts of our communities. We know that there are those who we consider outsiders who need to hear the good news from us, and we must be bold in sharing that good news with them.

We may think that our churches are totally different from those that came before us, but by studying the early church in Acts, we find they aren't so different after all.

Explore More

Acts 2:22-24

Fellow Israelites, listen to these words! Jesus the Nazarene was a man whose credentials God proved to you through miracles, wonders, and signs, which God performed through him among you. You yourselves know this. In accordance with God's established plan and foreknowledge, he was betrayed. You, with the help of wicked men, had Jesus killed by nailing him to a cross. God raised him up! God freed him from death's dreadful grip, since it was impossible for death to hang on to him.

Application

• The early Christ-followers needed to know the same truth we seek today. They needed to be reminded that Jesus was more than just a great teacher or a prophet, but was in fact the Son of God, the Messiah. They needed to be reminded that they contributed to the death of Jesus, through action or inaction, just like our sin separates us from Jesus who came to save us. However, not even death could separate us from Jesus; in the words of this Scripture: "It was impossible for death to hang on to him."

Questions

1. When have you been like the people talked about in this Scripture by either participating in acts of injustice or being silent in the face of injustice?
2. How does it feel to know that even those people who had Christ nailed to the cross would be offered forgiveness, and would be welcomed into the early church?
3. In your darkest moments, what can you do to remind yourself that Jesus has been through death and still wants a relationship with us and his church?

Acts 4:19-20

Peter and John responded, "It's up to you to determine whether it's right before God to obey you rather than God. As for us, we can't stop speaking about what we have seen and heard."

Application

• When Peter and John were being questioned, and were threatened if they didn't stop preaching the gospel, they found themselves in a precarious situation. They had to decide whether or not they were going to listen to the angry group telling them what to do or whether they would obey God. This is a place we often find ourselves. We don't necessarily have people telling us we can't talk about Jesus, but we have lots of people asking us to do the wrong thing. We have to make a choice—will we obey people or God?

Questions

1. Who are the people you listen to most in your life? Parents? Friends? Coaches or teachers? Why do you listen to them?
2. Have you ever had a time when you let someone convince you to do something you knew was a bad idea? Why were they so convincing?
3. When was a time that you resisted doing something because you knew it went against what God would want for you?

Made in the USA
Middletown, DE
30 January 2023

23557523R00042